CARING FOR HERSELF

Advice, activities, and more to help you care for your mental well-being

by Erin Falligant
illustrated by Brenna Vaughan

Published by American Girl Publishing

25 26 27 28 29 30 QP 10 9 8 7 6 5 4 3 2 1

No part of this book may be used or reproduced in any manner whatsoever without written permission except in the case of brief quotations embodied in critical articles and reviews.

Editorial Development: Jodi Goldberg, Mel Hammond, Barbara Stretchberry
Art Direction and Design: Kristi Lively, Valerie Paulin, Wendy Walsh
Illustrator: Brenna Vaughan
Production: Jodi Knueppel
Special thanks: Katie Hurley, LCSW, and Cara Natterson, MD

This book is not intended to replace the advice of or treatment by health-care professionals. It should be considered an additional resource only. Questions and concerns about mental or physical health should always be discussed with a doctor or other health-care professional.

Cataloging-in-Publication Data available from the Library of Congress

© 2025 American Girl and associated trademarks and trade dress are owned by American Girl, LLC. and ™ designate U.S. trademarks of American Girl, except as noted. American Girl ainsi que les marques et designs y afférents appartiennent à American Girl, LLC. et ™ désignent des marques de American Girl aux États-Unis, sauf indication contraire. Retain this address for future reference: American Girl, 333 Continental Blvd., El Segundo, CA 90245, U.S.A. Mattel Australia Pty. Ltd., 658 Church St., Richmond, Victoria, 3121. Mattel East Asia Ltd., 12/F, South Tower, World Finance Center, Harbour City, Tsimshatsui, HKSAR. Diimport & Diedarkan Oleh: Mattel Continental Asia Sdn Bhd. Level 19, Tower 3, Avenue 7, No. 8 Jalan Kerinchi, Bangsar South, 59200 Kuala Lumpur, Malaysia. Mattel South Africa (PTY) LTD, Office 102 I3, 30 Melrose Boulevard, Johannesburg 2196. GUARDAR PARA EVENTUAIS CONSULTAS. Distribuído por: Mattel do Brasil Ltda.- CNPJ : 54.558.002/0001-20 - Rua Verbo Divino, 1488 - 2º. Andar - 04719-904 - Chácara Santo Antônio - São Paulo - SP - Brasil. Serviço de Atendimento ao Consumidor: Contato: https://faleconosco.mattel.com.br/Contato. E-mail: sac.matteldobrazil@mattel.com. Importado y distribuido por: Mattel de México, S.A. de C.V., Miguel de Cervantes Saavedra No. 193, Pisos 10 y 11, Col. Granada, Alcaldía Miguel Hidalgo, C.P. 11520, México, Ciudad de México. R.F.C. MME-920701-NB3. Mattel Chile S.A., Pdte. Riesco 5561, Of. 203-204 PS2, Las Condes, Santiago. Mattel Argentina, S.A., Av. Libertador 1000, Piso 11 – Oficinas 109 y 111, Vicente López – Prov. Buenos Aires. Mattel Colombia, S.A., Calle 123#7-07 P.5, Bogotá. Mattel Perú, S.A., Av. Juan de Arona # 151, Centro Empresarial Juan de Arona, Torre C, Piso 7, Oficina 704, San Isidro, Lima 27, Perú. RUC: 20425853865. Reg. Importador: 02350-12-JUE-DIGESA. Marcas registradas utilizadas bajo licencia. Todos los derechos reservados. Imported by / Importé par: Mattel Canada Inc., Mississauga, Ontario L5R 3W2. Manufactured, imported, or distributed by: Mattel Europa B.V., Gondel 1, 1186 MJ Amstelveen, Nederland. Mattel U.K. Limited, The Porter Building, 1 Brunel Way, Slough SL1 1FQ, UK.

MO

MADE IN CHINA / FABRIQUÉ EN CHINE / HECHO EN CHINA / FABRICADO NA CHINA

Dear Reader,

You brush your teeth and hair. You exercise, feed your body what it needs, and get your zzz's to stay strong and healthy. But caring for yourself is about *more* than caring for your body. It's also about caring for your mind—your thoughts and feelings about yourself and the world around you.

The older you get, the more important it is to take care of both. Why? Because your body is changing and your world is, too. But when you're physically and mentally healthy, you can learn to work through hard things.

If you feel uncertain, sad, or are struggling with your feelings, you are not alone. You can learn how to manage your emotions and calm your worries. How to express yourself and ask for what you need. How to have better relationships with family and friends. How to feel confident at school, go after goals, and cope with challenges, knowing you'll make it through.

Caring for your mental health involves skill development in things like coping, asserting yourself, and understanding emotions. You can do things *right now* to feel better, stronger, and more confident. So what are you waiting for? Read on!

Your friends at American Girl

contents

healthy body, healthy mind

LOVE

so what is "mental health"?

By now, you know what physical health is all about. It's about taking care of your body, like eating well, being active, and getting enough sleep. But what is mental health, and why does it matter?

Mental health is about your *mind*—your thoughts and feelings, and how you express them. But it also affects your body. Did you know that stress and anxiety can give you a stomachache or a headache? When you're mentally healthy, you feel safe, loved, and good about yourself. You might have strong feelings, but you express them without hurting others. And even when life gets tough, you know you'll make it through.

Why does mental health matter?

Because how you feel and think about the world affects everything! It affects...

life at home with your family.

the friendships you make.

how you do at school.

how your body feels: how much energy or appetite you might have.

whether you go after your goals, like trying out for sports or a solo in a concert.

"Being resilient means when you get knocked down, you bounce right back up."

–Zmorah, Age 12

A strong, resilient girl . . .

- ☐ likes herself.
- ☐ feels loved by family and friends.
- ☐ can figure out what she's feeling or get help figuring it out.
- ☐ expresses feelings without hurting others.
- ☐ goes after her goals.
- ☐ believes she can do it!
- ☐ gives herself time to play and be creative.
- ☐ thinks positively about the future but . . .
- ☐ can bounce back when life gets hard.

How many boxes can you check today? No one can check all the boxes all the time. But just as you nurture your body when you're sick or injured, you can nurture your mental health. You can learn ways to boost your confidence, figure out your feelings, and feel more positive about the world around you. Ready to begin?

sleep and self-care

Did you know that when you care for your body, you're also caring for your mind? How much sleep you get, how active you are, and what you eat and drink *all* affect how you think and feel.

Get your zzz's

You know how it feels when you don't get enough sleep. It's hard to pay attention. You might feel grumpy or snap at a friend. So get those zzz's! Most kids your age need at least 9 or 10 hours a night. Creating a routine to help you get to sleep at night is called practicing *sleep hygiene*. Try these tips to get started:

Skip the caffeine. *Caffeine*—an ingredient found in chocolate and also many sodas, coffee drinks, and teas—can keep you up at night.

Stick to a schedule. Try to go to bed and wake up at the same time every day, even on the weekends. Your body will get used to the routine and it'll be easier to fall asleep.

Head outside. A little fresh air and exercise during the day makes it easier to sleep at night. Just try not to exercise right before bed if it gives you a burst of energy.

Power down. Put your phone and tablet away at least an hour before bedtime. The blue light plus the flickering screen images tell your brain to wake up instead of wind down.

Create a dream routine. Take a bubble bath, read a book, or listen to soft music. Do the same routine every night, and you'll feel sleepy when the time is right.

Get moving

One of the quickest ways to boost your mood is to move your body! Exercise helps your brain produce chemicals that make you feel happier. You don't have to be a star on the soccer field or spend an hour in PE class. Here are five ways to feel better in less than five minutes:

1. Dance to your favorite song.
2. Jump rope or hula hoop.
3. Make your bed as fast as you can.
4. Skateboard around the block.
5. Move your arms around in circles for one minute.

food affects mood

What you eat—and when—can affect how you feel. Say …

YES to nourishing your body. If you go too long without eating, your *blood sugar* drops. Blood sugar gives you energy, like gas in a car. If it drops too low, you might feel moody and have trouble concentrating. So eat three meals a day, and pack snacks.

YES to fruits, vegetables, proteins, and carbohydrates. If you don't get enough vitamins and minerals, it can affect your thinking, your mood, and how you feel overall.

YES to less sugar. Too many heavily sweetened foods in a day can leave you feeling anxious or crabby, or can make your energy jump up high and then crash down low.

YES to water. Staying well hydrated increases your energy and lifts your mood. Think about plants that don't get enough water: They look droopy!

YES to moderation. Your body and brain will feel their best if you find balance. So have the treat! But also eat the veggies. If you pay attention to how certain foods make you feel, you will get better at figuring out how to nourish your body.

Quiz

check your self-esteem

A big part of mental well-being is how you feel about yourself. Read each question. Which answer sounds most like you?

1. You're walking into school sporting new pink streaks in your hair. When your friend calls attention to them, you . . .

   a. say, "Yep, I wanted something different. I love them!"

   b. quickly change the subject so people stop looking at you.

   c. pull your hood over your head and hurry to the restroom to hide.

2. It's your first day at basketball camp, and your friend isn't there yet. You . . .

   a. introduce yourself to a girl who looks friendly.

   b. shoot a few hoops on your own, hoping someone comes up to you.

   c. ask your mom if you can wait in the car until your friend shows up.

3. Your gymnastics coach says she thinks you're ready for the competitive team. You . . .

a. sign right up. You can't wait to compete!

b. wonder if you should wait until next year. I mean, you'll be even better by then, right?

c. say nothing. You'll have your dad talk to your coach later to say you're definitely not ready.

4. A girl at school says your outfit looks babyish. You . . .

a. say, "Hey, thanks!" Then you hold your head high and walk right on by.

b. ignore her but vow never to wear the outfit again.

c. rush to your locker in tears. Can Mom bring you something new to wear like *right now*?

5. Your best friend is starting to hang out with a new girl at school. You . . .

a. try to get to know the new girl. Can you all be friends? The more, the merrier!

b. wonder what you did wrong. Why does your friend like the new girl more than she likes you?

c. give your friend the silent treatment. Hopefully she'll get the hint.

6. Your coach made you goalie for the first time, but a soccer ball just whizzed past you into the net. You . . .

a. remind yourself that you're still learning. You'll get the hang of it!

b. stick it out but secretly wish the game would end already.

c. ask your coach if someone else can play goalie. You don't want to lose the game for your team!

7. You wish you could sing a solo at the holiday concert. When your teacher asks for volunteers, you . . .

a. wave your hand wildly in the air.

b. wait for a moment, hoping your teacher has noticed your talent and will automatically choose you.

c. sit on your hands so that you don't volunteer and make a fool of yourself.

Answers

Mostly a's: Your self-esteem is **strong.** You know what you like and what you want, and you're not afraid to go after it! Keep caring for yourself, and give others encouragement when they need it, too.

Mostly b's: Your self-esteem could use a **boost.** Fear of failure gets in your way, and you don't always ask for what you want. Try stepping out of your comfort zone, and you'll soon feel better and stronger. You've got this!

Mostly c's: Low self-esteem is stopping you from seeing the unique, capable girl that you are. But just as you nurture a plant to help it thrive, you can **grow** your self-esteem. Start by treating yourself the way you want to be treated—with a little love, kindness, and respect.

confidence boosters

How do you gain more confidence and self-esteem? One step at a time. Here are three things you can do to give yourself a boost.

1. Stop unkind thoughts

When your self-esteem is low, you sometimes say unkind things to yourself. You focus on the negatives and make everything seem worse than it really is. So talk back to them. As soon as you hear that voice in your head, look in the mirror and try one of these:

- Say "PAUSE" out loud. Then say, "That's not true. The truth is . . ."
- Take a deep breath and say something positive about yourself.
- Give yourself a high five. Pairing positive thoughts with positive actions helps!

2. Practice kindness

Come up with messages you can tell yourself that are true and helpful.

- Instead of "You can't do that!" say, "Yes I CAN" or "Maybe I can't *yet*, but I'm learning."
- Instead of "You're going to mess up" say, "I might make a mistake, but that's OK. Everyone makes mistakes."
- Instead of "People are going to laugh at you" say, "If someone laughs, I'll survive. My friends and family will still love me."

3. Try something new

Confidence isn't just about telling yourself what you can do. Sometimes you have to *prove* it. How? By stepping out of your comfort zone and trying new things. Every time you do, you prove to yourself that you're brave. You remind yourself that it's OK to make mistakes (everyone does when they're learning something new!). And you grow your confidence, which will make trying the next new thing easier. Why wait? Try one of these right now:

- Learn a word in a foreign language.
- Try a food you've never eaten before.
- Learn a new dance.
- Style your hair in a new way.
- Play decorator and rearrange your room.
- Teach yourself a card trick.
- Learn how to write your name with your nondominant hand.

BIG truth

Confidence doesn't blossom overnight. It grows a little with every challenge you overcome and every new goal you set, big or small.

body love

Appreciating the skin you're in is a big part of mental well-being. How can you stay confident about your changing body and celebrate what's most unique about you? Try these six tricks.

1. Compliment yourself

When you look in the mirror, name three things you like, such as your freckles, the color of your eyes, and your strong arms. Then give yourself three compliments that have nothing to do with your looks. Are you hardworking? Kind? Creative?

2. Stop unkind thoughts in their tracks

If you start saying unkind things to yourself, *stop*. Would you talk to a friend like that? No way! Here's how to turn those thoughts around:

Be specific. Don't let one tiny thing affect how you feel about yourself. Instead of saying, "I look terrible!" try, "I don't love this headband" or "These aren't my favorite pants."

Try the "but I like" trick. If you have an unkind thought, add something positive. You might say, "I don't love this headband but I love the rest of my outfit!"

Remind yourself that you're about more than your looks. What skills do you have? What can your body do? Talents and skills make you much more interesting than how you do your hair or the clothes you wear.

3. Be smart about ads and videos

When you see a model or influencer who looks too perfect, remember there's no such thing as perfect. Influencers make things look easy, when they've actually recorded many takes to get the "perfect" photo or video! And photos of models in ads have been digitally touched up. Ask a parent or caregiver if you can write to companies to ask for ads showing *real* girls, just like you.

Body image

The way you feel about your body is called *body image*. Some people feel so pressured to look a certain way that it affects the way they eat, like skipping meals or only eating certain foods. If this is happening to you, talk to a trusted adult, such as a parent, caregiver, health-care provider, school counselor, or coach right away so they can get you the help you need.

4. Look around

Beauty comes in all shapes and sizes. Girls can be tall, small, or somewhere in between. Some are strong and love to play sports while others are creative and love to make works of art. Real beauty comes from being true to your passions and sharing them with confidence.

5. Be a role model

Rather than talking about dieting or weight with friends, talk about books, movies, sleepovers, and sports—topics you know make your friends feel happy and confident. Compliment them for what they can do rather than how they look. And when it comes to fashion, set your own trends. Wear what makes you feel good and confident. If you respect your own style, you'll show other girls how to respect themselves, too.

6. Post positive messages

Come up with kind words, such as "You're perfect just the way you are," "Be yourself," and "Love the skin you're in." Post them where you'll see them:

Print tiny messages on pencils with a fine-tip permanent marker.

Write messages on a mirror with an erasable marker.

Make posters for your bedroom walls or closet doors.

It’s about respect

If someone else makes inappropriate comments about your body, don’t be embarrassed. The other person should be ashamed, not you. Look them in the eye and say, “That’s not funny” or “That’s really immature.”

If they keep making comments—or if anyone *ever* touches you inappropriately—tell a parent, caregiver, teacher, or another adult you trust. It’s not your fault, and it’s not OK.

“If you feel uncomfortable because of someone else’s behavior, trust your gut. Don’t worry about hurting someone’s feelings. Tell an adult, and always put your health and safety first.”

—Gabby, **Age 14**

managing BIG emotions

figuring out all the feels

Part of caring for yourself is paying attention to your feelings. At your age, it's normal to feel strong emotions—and for them to change quickly. One moment you're happy. The next, you're caught up in a whirlwind of frustration or anger. Feelings can shift as quickly as the weather! Why? Because the hormones that cause changes in your body affect your *mood*, too. Combine that with the stress of changing friendships and keeping up with school, and it's no wonder your emotions feel mixed up sometimes.

Your changing emotions might feel out of control. But the more you pay attention to them, the more you'll understand them. *Meteorologists*, people who study the weather, can tell us when a storm is coming and how to ride it out safely. You can do the same with stormy emotions.

Have you ever felt different emotions at the same time? Maybe you were mad because your friend sat with someone else at lunch. But did you also feel hurt? Jealous? Scared that your friendship was changing? When you feel lots of emotions at once, it's hard to untangle them.

Try this:

Take a step back

When feelings come on strong, give yourself a break. If you're at school, head to the restroom. If you're at home, spend some time in your room. Sometimes you have to step out of a situation before you can see it clearly. Take a few deep breaths, and then ask yourself, "What am I feeling? And why?"

Talk to someone

Talk to a friend. Reach out to an older sibling, parent, or caregiver. Text your aunt or grandma. Even having a heart-to-heart with a pet or stuffed animal can help! Sometimes just saying what happened out loud helps you sort through how you feel—and can make you feel better.

Write in a journal

Open a notebook and jot down what you feel. Write as if you're talking to a friend. Start with the words "I feel SO ________ because ____________." Write as much as you want, as messy as you want. Then ask yourself, "What *else* could I be feeling?" Are there other emotions hiding below the surface? Tip: If writing feels like a chore, try using collage or drawing to represent your feelings in your journal. Art can be very calming!

expressing yourself

Once you figure out how you feel, it's OK to express yourself! When you were little, you expressed strong feelings by crying or throwing temper tantrums. Now that you're older, you know there are *better* ways that help the situation and don't hurt other people.

What helps and what hurts?

- Ignoring someone or sulking in silence HURTS. Other people can't read your mind. How can they help make things better if they don't even know what's wrong?

- Telling someone how you feel HELPS. It says that you trust them enough to be honest with them—and opens the door for them to share feelings with you, too.
- Trying to get other people on your side HURTS. It's OK to talk to someone else to help sort out what you feel, but don't expect them to take sides. That's not fair—and not helpful.
- Hollering or raising your voice HURTS. It's hard for someone to really hear your words when you're shouting, and you're more apt to say something you'll regret.
- Taking a break when you're angry or crying hard HELPS. Walk away until you feel like you can speak calmly and clearly.
- Being specific HELPS. Tell someone exactly what led to your strong feelings. Then tell them what you wish had happened instead.

Words that work

No matter what you're feeling, you can express yourself with a few simple words: "I feel ________ when you ________. I wish that you would ________________."

> **I feel hurt when you don't include me. I wish that you would invite me to come, too.**

These words are powerful! They put your feelings first but also let someone else know exactly how they can help make things better.

Be ready to listen

Saying what you feel doesn't automatically solve every problem. The person you're sharing with might have feelings of their own to share. It's hard to really listen when you're upset, but *try*—it might help you see what happened in a new way.

soothing yourself

Sometimes you have to sit with emotions until they fade away. Maybe you've tried talking them through, but you still feel blue. Maybe you reached out to a friend, but she's busy right now. What can you do to help yourself feel better? Plenty!

Quiet your mind

Clearing your mind and relaxing your body can calm big emotions. Try this:

Just breathe. Take three slow, deep breaths. Count to three as you breathe in. Hold your breath for three seconds. Blow it out, counting to three.

Flex and relax. Lie on your back and flex your muscles, one set at a time. Start with your face and neck, and move down to your shoulders and arms. Inhale, and then flex and hold your muscles (and your breath!) for five seconds. Exhale as you relax your body. Then move to the next set of muscles. Work your way from your head to your toes until your whole body feels soft and warm, like melted chocolate.

Take a mental trip. Close your eyes and picture yourself in a calm, relaxing place, like the beach or your favorite park. Imagine what you might see, hear, smell, and feel there. Can you take a trip to this calm place in your mind whenever you're upset or anxious?

Get creative

Express your emotions the way artists do. Write a poem about how you feel. Paint, color, draw, or even scribble your feelings on paper. Come up with new lyrics to your favorite song that tell the world how you feel—and then sing it at the top of your lungs.

Change the channel

See if you can switch from one emotion to another. Watch a funny video. Does it make you laugh? Play an upbeat song, and dance until the feel-good chemicals flow through your brain. Does it make you feel happier? Chances are, it will!

calming anxiety

Some emotions *don't* come and go—they stick with you for a while. Anxiety is like that. You might feel worried or nervous almost every day. You might get stomachaches before school. You might have trouble sleeping. Many kids feel this way—you're not alone! Tell a parent or caregiver, and try these exercises to help you feel better.

Examine your worries

Afraid that something bad will happen? Ask yourself this:

On a scale of 1 to 10, how likely is it that my worry will come true?

What is something good that could happen instead?

What would I say to a friend who was worrying about this?

Is this worry helping me or hurting me? *(List the ways it's helping and the ways it's hurting. Which list is longer?)*

Does anyone else worry about this? *(Hint: Ask a few good friends.)*

> "When you start to understand your fear, it loses its power. Once you say something aloud, it becomes much easier to deal with."
>
> —Gabby, Age 14

Face your fears

When you avoid something you're scared of, it might grow bigger and scarier. When you face it, it starts to shrink. Let's say you get nervous at sleepovers. Can you face that fear one step at a time?

Step 1: Make a list of places where you've spent the night, such as Grandma's, your cousin's, and your best friend's.

Step 2: Imagine yourself at each place. Which one makes you feel most anxious? Rewrite the list in order from the least scary situation to the most scary.

Step 3: Make plans to go to the first place on your list. Maybe you go to Grandma's house for a sleepover, but you make sure your mom keeps her phone on in case you need to come home. If you do? That's OK. Keep trying until you can make it through the night without anxiety getting the best of you. Then tackle the next place on your list. With every step you take, celebrate!

Ask for help

If your feelings of anxiety are making it hard for you to go to school or hang out with friends, let a parent, caregiver, or school counselor in on your worries. They can get you the help you need.

BIG truth

Every time you do the thing that scares you, you win. You prove that you're strong enough to stand up to your fear. And then? Your fear grows weaker and begins to fade away

handling panic attacks

Your heart pounds. You can't breathe. You're sweating and you feel sick or dizzy. What's happening?! It's not a heart attack, and you're not going to die. You might be having a panic attack. Many kids have them, and adults do, too. Panic attacks are no fun, but they do pass. And you can help them pass more quickly.

Why do they happen?

Something makes you anxious. Your brain tells your body that you're in danger, and your body releases a hormone called *adrenaline* that revs you up. It makes you stronger and faster so that you can fight or flee the danger. But when there's no *actual* danger, you have to tell your body it's OK to calm down.

5 ways to STOP a panic attack

Practice these exercises with a parent or caregiver:

1. **Take slow, deep breaths.** Breathe in as you count to three, hold your breath for three seconds, and breathe out as you count to five.
2. **Say something by heart.** A poem. Multiplication tables. Song lyrics. Giving your mind something to do helps relax your body.
3. **Look for the rainbow.** Search the room for something in every color: a red backpack, an orange shirt, a yellow stripe on the floor, and so on.
4. **Use your senses.** Name three things you can see, two things you can hear, and one thing you can feel.
5. **Imagine your happy place.** Close your eyes and picture yourself at the lake or lying in a pile of leaves, looking up at the sky. Imagine as many details as you can so that you really feel like you're there.

Play detective

When you've calmed down, try to figure out what caused the panic attack. Were you stressed about a big test? Worried about softball tryouts? A panic attack may be your body's way of saying, "I'm scared! Do something!" Ask yourself what's worrying you, and then do something about it. Call a study buddy, or practice with a teammate before tryouts. If you start feeling anxious again, reset your brain by practicing deep breaths and tuning in to your senses. You've got this!

BIG truth

Once you've successfully managed a panic attack, the next one won't be so scary.

feelings of depression

Do you feel sad, angry, or really tired almost every day? Are you having a hard time with homework? Are you eating more—or less—than usual? Are you having trouble falling or staying asleep? Do you feel like you just want to be alone a lot? Tell a parent or caregiver. These can all be symptoms of depression. Depression can be serious and often needs support from a doctor or therapist. Many kids are dealing with depression, but there are ways to help yourself feel better.

1. Listen to your thoughts

Depression is like constantly being followed by a rain cloud without an umbrella handy. Things can feel gloomy and overwhelming. You might think, *I don't have any friends*, even though you just got invited to a birthday party. You might miss a goal and think, *I can't do anything right!* even though the rest of the match went well. Nothing is ever *all* bad, even if it feels that way. Ask yourself this:

Is what I'm thinking true?

Try to prove that the thought is false.

Is it true that I can't do anything right? Not really. I'm pretty good at drawing.

Is what I'm thinking helping me or hurting me?

Make lists of how it helps you and hurts you. Which list is longer?

Actually, it hurts me when I tell myself I can't do anything right. It makes me want to stop trying. So what's the point in thinking it?

What is something I can tell myself instead?

I can remind myself that everyone makes mistakes, but I do lots of things right. And the more I practice, the better I'll get.

2. Stay off social media

If social media is making your feelings of sadness worse, staying off it can help. Try not to spend more than an hour a day online—or respect the limits your parents set for you. Focus on face-to-face friendships and connections instead.

3. Be kind to others

Experts say that being kind to someone else can make you feel happier. So compliment a teammate or friend on something they did well. Say thank you to your bus driver or teacher. Just smiling at someone prompts your brain to let positive emotions in. Do it enough, and you'll start to *feel* happier, too.

4. Start a gratitude journal

Every day, list three people or things you're thankful for. Some days it might be harder to think of them, but it'll get easier. And practicing being grateful can help you feel happier—it's a fact.

5. Ask for help

Depression can be tough to deal with on your own. Tell a parent or other adult how you feel, especially if . . .

- you're no longer interested in activities you once enjoyed.
- you feel hopeless.
- you're starting to take risks like drinking or doing drugs.

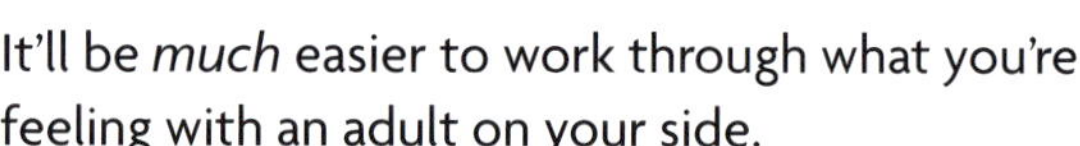

It'll be *much* easier to work through what you're feeling with an adult on your side.

BIG truth

No one feels happy all the time. That's just not possible. Some days, you're going to feel sad, worried, mad, or frustrated. But focusing on the positives—the people and things you're grateful for—can help you deal with tough emotions and keep you moving forward.

Tell someone!

If you *ever* have thoughts of hurting yourself, tell someone right away. Tell . . .

- a parent or caregiver.
- an aunt or uncle.
- a teacher.
- a coach.
- a friend's parent.
- a grandparent.
- a neighbor.
- a school counselor.
- a doctor.

There are so many people in your life who want to be there for you! Things may feel hopeless right now, but you won't always feel this way. Tough times don't last forever. Whatever you're going through, with the right support in place, things *will* get better.

connecting with family & friends

relationships at home

Caring for yourself also means caring for your relationships with family, which can look different for everyone. When you feel safe and loved by the people closest to you, it's easier to handle whatever comes your way.

Go-to family members

How does your family look out for you? Maybe your grandma comes to your soccer games. Maybe your cousin taught you a new dance. Maybe your stepdad picks you up from school. Think about the family members you reach out to when you . . .

- get sick or hurt.
- have great news to share.
- need help with homework.
- have a fight with a friend.
- want to learn something new.
- feel bored.
- have questions about your changing body.
- need to solve a problem.
- have a big game or concert coming up.

Be a go-to person!

The older you get, the bigger the role you play in your family. Maybe you …

- babysit a younger sibling.
- walk the dog or scoop the cat litter.
- ask a parent how their day was when they walk in the door.
- invite a sibling to play a game when they're bored or lonely.
- help with dinner or dishes.
- clean not just your room, but other parts of the house, too.
- make cards or little gifts when someone needs a pick-me-up.

In the same way that you care for yourself, you care for your family. Because you know that when you stick together and look out for one another, you're all a little stronger.

When a parent can't parent

Sometimes parents just aren't able to care for their kids. Maybe they suffer from mental illness. Maybe they're addicted to drugs or alcohol. Maybe they learned to parent from their parents, who weren't very present either. If this is true for your parent, remember this:

- **You didn't do anything wrong.** Even if your parent hollers at you or says hurtful things, this isn't your fault.
- **You have a right to feel safe.** If you're scared or hurt, talk to an adult you trust right away. That's the best way to protect yourself—and to find help for your parent.
- **Things can get better.** With treatment and support, your parent *can* get healthier. Until then, rely on the many people who care about you to help you through.

family talk

As you get older, you might crave more choices and freedom. You might also have new worries, or questions about your body. Here's how to start conversations that can help you get the support you need *without* frustration, anger, or arguing.

Pick the right time

Don't start a conversation when you're upset or tired. And try not to talk when time is tight, like while you're rushing to get ready for school. Instead, pick a time when you know you're already spending time together, like in the car or while helping with dinner. If you can't think of a good time, let your parent know you'd like to talk about something. Then ask if you can set up an "appointment" for later.

Use words that work. Remember the powerful little words "I feel . . ." Start with your feelings, and then ask for what you want or need. Be specific!

I feel embarrassed because I think I need a bra, but I don't have one yet. Can we go shopping?

I feel left out because my friends all have pierced ears. Can we talk about when you think I'll be ready?

I feel stressed out because I don't have enough time for homework. Can we make my bedtime a little later?

Keep it simple. Instead of bringing up a lot of things all at once, focus on the *one* thing that's most important to you right now. You don't have to tackle all your wants or worries in one conversation. If this talk goes well, it'll set the stage for many more to come.

Take a break if you need to. If you feel like you might say something hurtful, ask for a time-out. Say, "I'm starting to feel upset. Can we talk again later?" That shows you're mature enough to tune in to your feelings and take care of them.

Give them time to think. If you're asking for something, don't demand an answer right away. Ask if you can talk more tomorrow or over the weekend. Then stick to that agreement. If you give your parent or caregiver a little space, there's a better chance they'll find a way to meet you in the middle.

Sibling spats

Sometimes your sibling might feel like your best friend. Other times? Your worst enemy. When that happens, a few words go a long way. Try these:

I don't like fighting with you.

Can we make up? I'm ready to talk.

I'm sorry we fought. How can we make things better?

Sometimes you don't need words at all. A smile, a hug, or a (kind) joke can pave the way back to good.

healthy friendships

When you're taking good care of yourself, you surround yourself with friends you can count on. They may go to your school, or they may not. They may be your age, or they may be a little older or younger. They may be far away. They may be family. They may even be furry! (Pets make the *best* listeners.) Just make sure they care about you and bring out the best in you.

6 signs of a good friend

A good friend . . .

1. is happy when life goes your way and upset for you when it doesn't.
2. really listens when you have something to say.
3. doesn't talk badly about you—ever.
4. stands up for you if someone hurts you.
5. lets you have other friends without getting mad or jealous.
6. apologizes when she needs to—and is willing to forgive *you*, too.

Do you have friends like that? Cherish and protect those friendships. Be as good a friend to them as they are to you.

Am I a good friend?

See how many of these statements sound like you.

- ☐ When I tell a friend I'm going to do something, I do it.
- ☐ I stand up for my friends if someone else treats them badly.
- ☐ I try to be myself around my friends. That way, they can get to know the real me!
- ☐ I don't say mean things to my friends or about my friends.
- ☐ If I'm upset with a friend, I talk to her instead of talking behind her back.
- ☐ If a friend is hard on herself, I try to boost her up.
- ☐ I ask my friends when I need help or support. I don't expect them to guess.
- ☐ If I hurt a friend, I apologize right away.

feeling lonely or left out

Maybe you're staring at your phone or tablet, waiting (and waiting and waiting . . .) for a friend to get back to you. Maybe your two good friends are doing something without you. Feeling lonely or left out hurts, but you can turn that feeling around.

Watch your thoughts. Swap out words like never, always, and everyone for less extreme words.

My friends **never** call or text me back!

*Actually, they **usually** do, if I'm patient.*

My friends **always** do things without me.

*Well, they **sometimes** do, but I hang out with other friends, too.*

Everyone likes the new girl better than me.

__Lots__ of people like her. And lots of people like me. It's not a competition.

Admit you can't read minds. If a friend doesn't get back to you right away, don't assume she's ignoring you or suddenly likes you less. Instead . . .

- come up with two other explanations. Is she doing chores? Or visiting her grandma?
- find out! Call or message her and ask her what she's up to.
- don't wait around for a response. Get busy! Clean your room, dance, or teach your pup a trick. That way, when your friend asks what *you're* up to, you'll have an answer.

Stay open. If your best friend is hanging out with someone else . . .

- let her know you're feeling left out. It's OK to ask for some one-on-one time.
- don't force her to choose between her new friend and you. There's no law that says she can have only one friend (and *psst* . . . you're allowed to have other friends, too).
- get to know the new girl. Can the three of you hang out? You might feel uncomfortable at first, but she might, too. Focus on making her feel included, and you might forget that you ever felt left out.

Make a new friend. If you're feeling lonely more than you'd like, try to widen your friendship circle. Where can you meet someone new?

- Step outside—outside your room, outside your house, outside your comfort zone. Meeting someone new is a lot more likely if you're willing to *do* something new.
- Join band or a sport. You'll meet lots of girls at practice, and you may end up with a whole new group of friends you can rely on.
- Join a club. Girl Scouts, 4-H, a book club, a gaming club—they all count! Getting together with kids who like the same thing you do is a great way to meet a good friend.

it's ok to disagree

Friends don't always agree on everything—that's just not possible. In a healthy friendship, you're allowed to say what you think, even if your friend feels differently. She's allowed, too! But if you start butting heads, try to calm down and hear her point of view.

When someone disagrees with you

- **Take a breath.** Then say, "Tell me why you feel that way." Try to really listen, without interrupting. If you hear her out, she'll be more likely to listen when it's your turn to talk.
- **Use reassuring words.** Instead of jumping right in to disagree, let her know you've heard her. Say, "That's a good point" or "I never thought about it that way."
- **Start with "I."** When it's your turn to talk, say, "I feel . . ." or "I think . . ." If you start with the word "You," your friend might feel like you're pointing your finger at her or accusing her of something. She might stop listening or turn away.
- **Take a break.** If you start getting angry or upset, ask for a break. It's better to walk away for a while than to say something you'll regret.

- **Meet in the middle.** You and your friend might not agree on everything, but you probably agree on a lot of things. Just saying, "I agree with that" shows your friend you can meet her halfway.
- **Agree to disagree.** If you talk things through and still disagree, that's all right. You've probably learned a few things about each other, right? So smile and say, "Let's agree to disagree on that." Give your friend a hug, and then move on.

> "When I disagree with a friend, I talk to myself. I explain my side of the story, and then I pretend to be their lawyer and defend them. Afterward, I can usually see my friend's point of view."
> –Ellianna,
> Age 11

BIG truth

It's OK to disagree. It's *not* OK to treat someone badly just because they have a different point of view.

standing up to bullying

Mean comments, teasing, threats—it's all bullying, and it's all wrong. If it's happening to you, know that you *will* get through this. Here's how to take care of yourself:

- **Don't bully back.** You'll just fuel the fire and keep the fight going. Instead . . .
- **Look for helpers.** Are there friends who can be with you in the hallway, lunchroom, locker room, or wherever the bullying is happening?
- **Speak up.** If you can, try little words with big power:

  "Wow, that was immature."

  "Thanks!" (A little humor can throw someone off guard.)

  "Whatever."

  "What?" (Pretend you can't hear. Repeat the word as many times as you need to.)

  "Uh-huh."

  "Really?"

- **Record the bullying.** If the mean behavior continues, write down what's been happening and how you've handled it. Then talk to a parent, caregiver, teacher, principal, or other trusted adult. Take your notes with you. Take a friend, too, if it helps.
- **Be kind to yourself.** It can take time for the bullying to end, but eventually, it will. Meanwhile, take extra good care of yourself and lean on your friends and family. Remind yourself that this *isn't* your fault. You didn't cause the bullying, but you were brave enough to stand up to it.

Cyberbullying

If someone threatens or embarrasses you online, follow these dos and don'ts:

DO ask a parent or caregiver to take a photo of the bullying with their phone or other device.

DO ask a parent or caregiver for help deciding what to do. Can you block the bully from contacting you or commenting on your posts?

DO report the bullying if it continues. You can report it directly to your school and to social media sites.

DON'T feel ashamed. The only way to stop cyberbullying is to speak up.

DO take a break from your phone or tablet. Unplug and focus on face-to-face time with friends instead.

Quiz

time to log out?

Watching videos, playing games, messaging with friends . . . Time on your phone or tablet can be a fun way to connect with friends and explore the world. But too much time online means you might be missing out on *real* life.

Is it time to log out? Take this quiz to find out. Check every statement that sounds like you.

- ☐ When I don't have a device in my hands, my thumbs twitch. I need something to hold, tap, or scroll.
- ☐ When I get together with friends, we spend more time staring at our screens than talking to each other.
- ☐ I hear imaginary dings constantly. (Was that my tablet? Nope. Wait, was that my phone?)
- ☐ I get my best exercise wandering around the house in my virtual reality headset. (I get a few bruises that way, too.)
- ☐ I've taken at least one ridiculous challenge I saw in a video, even though the voice in my head said, *Stop! Don't do it!*
- ☐ I study emojis in messages, trying to figure out what my friends are *really* saying.
- ☐ A dead battery in my device can ruin my whole day!
- ☐ I play video games when I'm supposed to be doing homework (but that's OK, because I'm great at doing more than one thing at a time).
- ☐ I've gotten in trouble with my friends for saying something in a message or post that I shouldn't have. Oops!
- ☐ I fall asleep at night to a glowing screen. It makes for a great night-light though, right?

Answers

If you checked **3 or fewer boxes,** good for you! You log in just enough to play a few games or watch a few videos. But you log out when you need to, like for homework, sleep, and face-to-face time with friends.

If you checked **4 to 6 boxes,** your device is starting to take over your life. It's time to set limits so that you can get enough sleep, focus when you need to, and keep your *real-life* relationships healthy and strong.

If you checked **7 or more boxes,** drop your phone or tablet and slowly step away . . .

Turn the page for tips on how to take back control of your life—and what could happen if you *don't*.

Warning! If you spend too much time on your devices, you can feel . . .

lonely. Messaging friends and playing games with them online isn't the same as hanging out in person. There's no substitute for looking a friend in the eye, talking, and laughing with them.

depressed. Seeing photos or videos of people who can dance, style their hair, or dress perfectly can make you feel less happy with your own life.

stiff and achy. Too much time sitting in one position isn't great for your body. Staring at a screen can lead to headaches, too. What's better? Getting up, moving your body, and stepping outside.

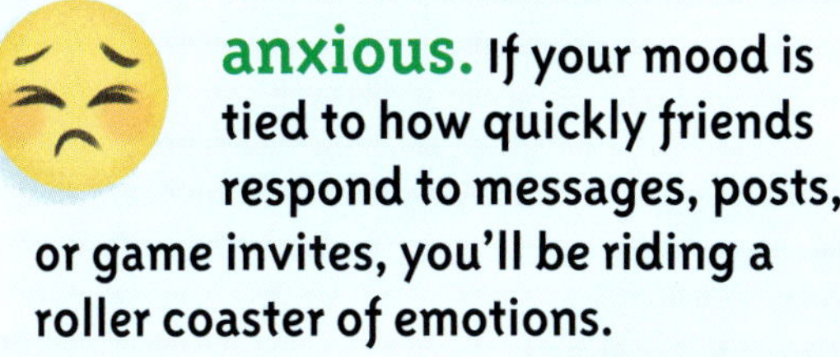

anxious. If your mood is tied to how quickly friends respond to messages, posts, or game invites, you'll be riding a roller coaster of emotions.

distracted. How can you focus on other things when you're constantly checking your phone?

tired. If you're swiping instead of sleeping, you'll run out of steam. And a tired girl can feel even *more* distracted, anxious, and depressed.

BIG truth

YOU control how much you let screen time and social media affect your day, your mood, and your life.

Take control

Cut down on screen time. (It's better than quitting cold turkey, right?) Check your screen use and then set a timer or the app control settings for half that amount.

See how you feel. If you start feeling anxious or upset, *log out*. Don't wait around for friends to respond or waste time playing a game that frustrates you.

Turn off notifications. Or set your phone to airplane mode so you're not flooded with posts, messages, and invites all day. You won't miss a thing—you'll see it all when you log back in.

Be choosy. Unfollow strangers and people who say things online that upset you. We can't always control who we connect with in real life, but online, we *can*.

Make a plan. What will you do when you feel the urge to grab your device? Dance it out? Doodle in a notebook? It'll be tough at first, but it'll get easier. You'll start to remember the many other ways you can spend time and connect with friends.

Declare a Screen-Free Day

Pick one weekend day when you won't log in to any devices. Challenge your family and friends to try it, too. How will you spend the oodles of time you free up?

self-care
to do

at (and after) school

watch your schedule

It's hard to take care of yourself when you have too many things packed into each day. It's like a bucket of water. If you keep adding cup after cup of water, your bucket will overflow!

How do you know when you have too much going on? You might . . .

- feel tired all the time.
- have trouble sleeping.
- get stomachaches and headaches.
- have difficulty concentrating in class.
- miss school because you're not feeling well.
- be really cranky, snapping at people or bursting into tears without knowing why.

Sound like you? Here's how to free up some space:

Write it all down. Use a whiteboard, poster board, computer, or tablet to map out your schedule for the week. Include school, sports, music lessons, and so on. Block off time for homework, chores, eating, sleeping, and showering. How much white space is left? You should see at least a small patch every day.

Let it go. Sometimes you can let go of activities that stress you out or that you no longer enjoy. Ask yourself, "Do I still look forward to it?" and "Could I take a break?"

Talk to your parents or caregiver. Ask if you can take a break from those activities. You may need to wait until the end of a season or semester. But knowing you can stop sometime soon might lessen some of your stress right now.

feeling lost in class?

Ask for help! The sooner, the better. And don't feel ashamed about it. Getting help doesn't mean you're less smart than anyone else. In fact, asking for help is the *smartest* thing you can do.

Ask right away

If you get confused, ask your teacher for help during class, right after, or first thing the next morning. Teachers want you to do well. They respect kids who aren't afraid to say they need a little extra help.

Be kind to yourself

If you're saying this: **Try this instead:**

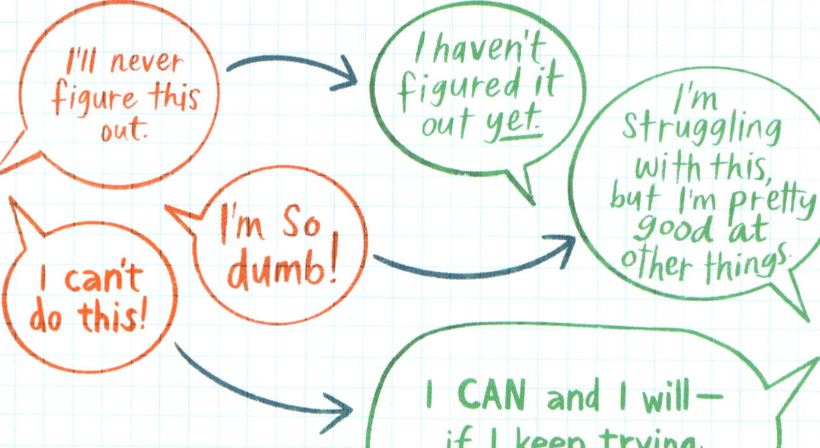

Celebrate small steps

When you figure something out or do well on a quiz, give yourself a BIG pat on the back. Remember that success the next time you're feeling lost or confused. It'll make it easier to ask for help again when you need to.

Look for experts

Everyone is an expert at something. Does your sibling binge-watch history documentaries? Is your mom a math whiz? Does your cousin love doing science experiments? Lean on them! Ask if they will be your go-to people for help in those subjects. Also see if your school has programs for extra teacher support or peer tutors available.

Find study buddies

Exchange phone numbers with friends in your class. If you get confused while doing homework, call them. Study for quizzes together at recess or lunchtime, too.

BE THE TUTOR

Is a friend or sibling struggling with something you do well? Give them tips! We all need a helping hand sometimes, and you can offer one just as often as you ask for one.

making the grade

Are you feeling pressure to get straight A's? That's a lot to live up to! If trying to make perfect grades is making you miserable, ask yourself where the pressure is coming from.

If you feel pressure from your parents or caregiver

- Find the right time to talk to them. Don't bring up grades when you're frustrated with homework or bummed about getting a lower grade than you hoped for. Set up a time to talk later—maybe while making dinner or taking a walk.
- Say, "I feel pressure to get straight A's, and it's stressing me out," or "I want to get good grades, but I want to enjoy my classes, too."
- Ask if there are some subjects your parents or caregiver think are more important to do well in than others. If you study hard in social studies, can you focus on having fun with coding?
- Make a pact with your parents or caregiver. Instead of asking what score you got on a test or assignment, maybe they can ask, "What did you learn?" or "What did you enjoy most?" Then be prepared to answer!

BIG truth

Flaws make you human and lovable. Let people see the perfectly imperfect you!

If you're putting the pressure on yourself

- Ask why. Do you take pride in being the "smart one" in class? Are you trying to do everything perfectly? Remember that perfect isn't possible, and pushing for it will only wear you out.
- If you catch yourself saying, "I have to get done before anyone else," or "I have to get the best score," ask what will happen if you don't. Will the sky fall? Will you fail the class? Will kids think you're not very smart? Nope. A single test score will never determine your whole grade—or how smart you are.
- Do something every day that won't be graded. Learn a new dance. Make clay pots. Look for animal shapes in the clouds. Just have fun!

in the spotlight

Lots of kids have performance anxiety when they're in front of a crowd. It can strike when you're singing onstage, doing a gymnastics routine, or even giving a report at school. Performance anxiety is perfectly normal, but it's no fun. The good news? There are ways to deal with it. Try these dos and don'ts:

Before the event

DO watch your words. Instead of saying, "I'm going to freak out!" tell yourself, "I might feel anxious, but that's OK. There are ways I can calm myself down and keep going."

DO imagine everything going well. If you're about to do a routine on the bars, close your eyes and picture your teammates smiling at you. Feel the bar in your hands, and imagine performing your very best routine, right down to the cheer of the crowd when you're done.

DON'T avoid other people. Look for a teammate who seems as nervous as you, and crack a joke about the butterflies in your belly. You'll worry less and feel stronger together.

"If I get nervous before a gymnastics meet, I tell myself it doesn't matter if I win or lose. I should just try to have fun!"

—Kenley, **Age 11**

During the event

DO make friends with *adrenaline*, that hormone your body releases when you're nervous. Adrenaline gives you energy and helps you focus. Your heart beats faster, your palms sweat, and butterflies fill your stomach. When you feel those things, tell yourself, "Good. That means it's go time. My mind and body are ready."

DON'T let mistakes paralyze you. Move on to your next skill or the next line of your report, and keep going.

Afterward

DON'T focus on scores. Your goal was to stay calm and not let the pressure get to you. So if you kept your cool, you scored big!

If you did panic? Pat yourself on the back for surviving the situation, and set your sights on what you'll do next time.

BIG truth

Success is never about a single event, game, or performance. And panicking doesn't mean you failed. The only way to fail is to give up and stop trying.

trying new things

Sports and activities you've never tried before can feel scary. You might wonder, *What if I make a mistake?* or *What if I mess up in front of everyone?* But trying new things is also a great way to build confidence and make new friends. Are you going to let the "what ifs" get in the way of that? Nope. Here's how to push past them.

Add the word "so" to "what if."
So what if you mess up? No one rocks anything the first time she tries it. Or the second. Or the third. The only way to get better is to try. If you mess up, you might be embarrassed for a few seconds, but you'll get over it—guaranteed.

Focus on the positives. Think of all the good things that could happen. What if you learn new skills? What if you have a blast? What if you make new friends?

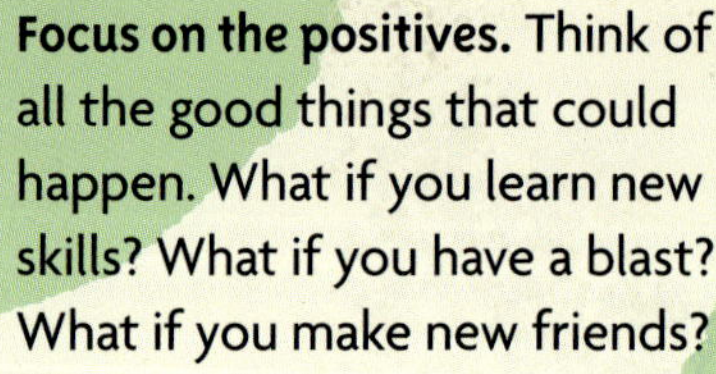

Accept mistakes. You're going to make them—that's how you learn. You knew this as a little kid. When you learned to ride a bike, you fell, got back up, and tried again. Every time, you got better and went farther. Every mistake gets you one step closer to success.

Shake them off. If you do mess up in front of everyone? Move on. Compliment someone else on how she's doing—right away. If you don't draw attention to your mistakes, other people will forget them. They'll only remember how supportive you were.

Name three. After trying something new, think of three good things that happened. Did you keep going, even when things got tough? Did you learn something? Did you have fun?

Ask for help. Feeling like you'll never get it? Remind yourself that you just can't do it *yet*. Ask for tips from a coach or a friend, and really listen. If one tip doesn't work, try another.

Make a mistake—on purpose!

Take a video of yourself doing a dance before you know all the moves. Splatter paint on your artwork and turn the mistake into a masterpiece. Why? It'll prove that the sky won't fall. Good things can come from mistakes. Once you see that, you'll worry way less about making them in the future.

coping with change

bouncing back

Life is full of changes and challenges that you didn't expect—from changes in your family to illness and injuries. But if you take care of yourself, you can become more *resilient*.

What is resilience? It's being able to . . .

- handle whatever life throws at you—to keep going and keep trying, even when things are tough.
- stand up for yourself, hold your head high, and *know* you'll make it through.
- come out the other side with new skills to handle the next big challenge.

Being resilient is like being a rubber band. You might get stretched by stressful or uncomfortable situations, but you bounce right back.

Quiz

how resilient are you?

Answer these questions to find out.

1. Your mom just got a new job, and you may have to move! What happens next?

   a. You slam your bedroom door and holler through the crack that you're not going *anywhere*.

   b. You call a good friend, tell her the news, and brainstorm ways you can stay in touch.

2. You sprain your ankle right before the school dance. What happens next?

   a. You ditch the dance and stay home to mope.

   b. You choose a bandage that matches your new outfit, grab your crutches, and go!

3. Your best friend tells you she needs some space. What happens next?

   a. You storm off in a huff and declare the friendship over. Who needs a friend like that anyways?

   b. You give her space, even though it's hard, and then reach out to a new girl you've been wanting to get to know.

4. Your dad tells you that he's getting remarried. What happens next?

   a. You vow not to go to the wedding. You're still hoping your mom and dad will get back together!

   b. You ask your new stepmom-to-be if you can help with the wedding. Maybe it'll be fun!

5. You're usually a striker, but your coach suddenly wants you to play goalie. What happens next?

   a. You pretend to get hurt so that you can sit out the rest of the season.

   b. You ask your coach for some tips, get out on the field, and do your best.

6. You got assigned to a new cabin at camp, and you don't know a soul. What happens next?

   a. You lie low and pretend to be really into the zipper of your backpack.

   b. You look for someone who seems just as lonely as you and go sit by her.

7. During a storm, your bedroom floods and needs to be renovated. What happens next?

   a. You can't stop the flood of tears. What if your new room isn't the same?

   b. You pull out your sketchbook and start figuring out how you're going to redecorate.

Answers

If you answered mostly **a's,** change sometimes gets the best of you. If you answered mostly **b's,** you know the number-one secret of resilience: You can't always control what happens to you, but you *can* control how you react to it.

How? By talking back to negative thoughts. By looking for the good in every situation. By learning from (and sometimes laughing at) your mistakes. By asking for help when you need it, and by looking for ways to help others, too.

BIG truth

Life is going to change. It's how you react to those changes—what you do next—that counts. And there's *always* something you can do to make a new situation feel better.

Being the new girl

New team? New school? New neighborhood? At some point, you'll find yourself alone in a new place, without a familiar face in sight. When that happens, take a deep breath and try to meet someone new.

Three ways to make a friend:

- **Just say hello.** Do you see someone who looks as lonely as you feel? Go up to her and say hello. Add, "I just moved here," or "This is my first day."
- **Ask for help.** Asking someone how to find a classroom or the water fountain could lead to a new friendship!
- **Offer a compliment.** Tell someone you like her scrunchie, her bike, or the doodle she's drawing.

The conversation might feel awkward at first, but give it time. Some girls come out of their shells more slowly than others. You can't force new friendships, but there's a lot you can do to nurture them.

getting sick or hurt

Injuries and illnesses can be scary. But you've gotten sick and hurt in the past, right? You survived those times, and you'll get through this, too.

Feel what you feel. You might feel scared. You might be worried about the things you're missing out on. You might feel jealous that friends can do things you can't do. Give yourself time to feel all those emotions. And then?

Think of all you *can* do. If you're sick, can you eat as many ice pops as you want? Binge-watch your favorite shows or stay in your jammies all day? If you're hurt, can you still attend your team's games as a cheerleader?

Try something new. If you hurt your ankle and can't play soccer for a month, ask your parents if you can swim instead.

Give it a rest. Listen to your body and rest when you need to. Giving yourself downtime helps you bounce back.

"I bruised a bone in my knee. I thought I'd be off gymnastics for a week, but it ended up being *four* weeks. I was disappointed, but I used the downtime to catch up on reading."
—Victoria, Age 10

Ask for help. Can a friend bring your homework? Can a family member show you how to use crutches without getting sore arms? Lean on the people you love. They want to help!

Celebrate small steps. Can you do something today you couldn't do a couple of days ago? Celebrate that! It's proof that you're moving in the right direction.

Chronic illness

Some illnesses, like asthma, diabetes, and epilepsy, are *chronic*, which means they last a long time or even a lifetime. If you're diagnosed with one, you might feel sad and scared. Here's how to take charge and feel better:

- **List your questions.** Then ask your parents and doctor to help answer them. The more you know, the more in control you will feel.
- **Connect with kids who have the same illness.** Ask your parents to help you look for support groups, or sign up for a walk or run raising money for a cure. You'll see that many kids are dealing with this—you're not alone.
- **Be honest.** If someone asks about your illness, tell them how it affects you and how it doesn't. Most people with chronic illness lead very full lives, and you will, too.

changing friendships

Does your best friend not want to be friends anymore? Ouch! Losing a good friend really hurts, but you'll get through this. You can't control how your friend feels, but you *can* control how you react.

Don't say something you'll regret. Be polite to your friend, and treat yourself well, too—don't bully yourself with mean thoughts. People change over time and so do friendships. You have no reason to feel ashamed if a friendship ends.

Let yourself feel sad. There's no way around it—you can't fast-forward through grief like you can through a song or video. So do what you need to do: cry, curl up with a parent or a pet, or listen to music.

Focus on your fans. Write down everyone who cares about you: siblings, parents, caregivers, cousins, teammates, classmates, neighbors, aunts, uncles, and grandparents. Include pets, too. Now circle the people you consider friends. Family can be friends. Grown-ups can be friends. Pets can be friends. When you see how many friends you have, you'll feel more lucky than lonely.

Make a new friend. Invite someone at school to eat lunch with you. Ask a teammate to partner up for a drill. Welcome a new neighbor by asking her to hang out. Some new friendships will fit like a glove, and others won't. But keep trying. There's always a new friendship around the corner, if you're willing to look for it.

Crushed by a crush

It's a different kind of heartbreak from losing a friend, but you bounce back the same way:

1. Don't plead, be mean, or try to change your crush's mind. Just walk away with your head held high, knowing you'll get through this.
2. Let yourself feel sad for as long as you need to. Then . . .
3. Get busy feeling better. Step outside. Be active. Make plans with a friend. You'll feel happy again someday soon, but you don't need a new crush to get you there. Resilient girls create their own happiness.

BIG truth

Having one best friend isn't the secret to happiness. Many girls feel happier when they're surrounded by a few good friends instead.

dealing with divorce

If you find out your parents are splitting up, you might feel a tidal wave of sadness, anger, and fear. It's important to feel those emotions—and to express them. It might feel like the future is one big question mark. But many kids have survived divorce, and you and your family will, too, one day at a time.

Know this:

The divorce is NOT your fault. Nothing you said or did caused this. No child has ever been responsible for her parents' divorce—period.

If your parents are fighting, that's NOT your fault either. Put on your headphones and listen to music or your favorite book. Take the dog for a walk. If you're feeling overwhelmed, talk with a trusted adult, teacher, school counselor, coach, doctor, or therapist.

You CAN'T fix this. If you're dreaming up ways to get your parents back together, *stop*. That only works in the movies, not in real life!

You WON'T lose one of your parents. You'll spend time with both of them.

You DON'T have to pick sides, no matter what anyone says. You might spend more time at one house than the other, but you can keep loving both parents equally.

Do what you can

If you have questions, ask. Your parents might not have all the answers right now, but they'll be able to answer some questions. Talk to friends who have been there, too. Bringing your worries out into the open will help you feel better.

Make a plan. Ask your parents if you can create a calendar showing which house you'll stay at on which night. Keep it on your phone and post it on the refrigerator at both houses. When you know where you'll be and when, you'll feel more confident and in control.

Make a list of things that *aren't* changing, such as sports, sleepovers with friends, and hobbies. See how much of your world will stay the same?

Look for the positives

Can you decorate your room in both houses?

Will you get special one-on-one time with each parent?

Will you meet new friends now that you'll have another neighborhood to call your own?

BIG truth

You couldn't keep your parents from falling out of love, and you can't make them fall back into love. But you can control how you deal with the divorce. Remind yourself that you won't always feel this way. Things *will* get easier.

adjusting to a new marriage

Maybe you've gotten used to your parents being divorced. But when a parent remarries, it can feel like being thrown back into rough waters. Here are questions many girls have—and answers to help you stay afloat.

Q: Why do I feel so sad?

A: A new beginning means the end of something else. Maybe you were hoping your parents would get back together. But letting go of that idea frees up space in your head and heart. Let yourself feel sad, and then let it go—like a balloon. Once you do, you'll feel more ready to move forward.

Q: Will I still have one-on-one time with my parent?

A: Yes, and it's OK to ask for it. Plan special time for the two of you every week. Once you make those plans, you'll feel better about the time you'll be sharing with your stepparent and stepsiblings.

Q: Does liking my stepparent mean I'm disloyal?

A: Absolutely not! You can like or even love a stepparent and still be loyal to your mom or dad. A stepparent will never replace a parent—it's a different relationship. But if you stay open, it can be strong and loving, and you'll have one more person looking out for you.

Q: Is my parent going to love my stepsiblings as much as me?

A: Your parent will care about your stepsiblings, just as you might begin to care about your stepparent. But that doesn't mean he or she will love you any less. It doesn't work that way. Caring for step-kids won't change how your parent feels about you—not ever.

Q: Will I have to share a room?

A: Maybe, but focus on the positives. Can you and your stepsibling have fun redecorating? Will it take half the time to clean your room now? If you want more privacy, hang a curtain—then open it when you want to be together. Chances are good that eventually, you will.

Q: What if we don't feel like a "family"?

A: You won't at first—that'll take time. One day, you'll realize it's getting easier. There'll be ups and downs, but that's true in any family. There'll be fights and frustrations, but there'll be more laughter and love, too.

"Families change, but nothing will change your parents' love for you. New people may join your family, but that just means you'll have more people who love and care about you!"

—Gabby,
Age 14

losing someone you love

Oof. Your heart might feel shattered into a million pieces. You might think you'll never be happy again. Grieving hurts—there's no way around it. But you *will* make it through.

Feel what you feel. It's OK to . . .

cry.

be angry at the person you lost because they left you.

be relieved because your loved one isn't suffering anymore.

smile at memories of the one you lost.

forget your loss for a while and laugh.

feel numb—or feel nothing at all. It doesn't mean you love the person any less.

want to go on with life as usual. Your normal routine might be comforting for you right now.

Say what you feel. Talk with family, friends, or a counselor. Join a support group for kids who lost someone they love. If you're not ready to talk yet, that's OK. But there are many people who'll be there for you when you are.

Get creative. Express your feelings by writing a poem or song. Draw, journal, or make an album filled with photos of your loved one.

Share memories. Don't be afraid to talk about the person you lost. It'll remind you of all the memories you'll *never* lose. You might laugh at the memories, or you might cry. That's all part of grieving, and it'll help you heal.

Write a letter. Tell your loved one what you miss and what you'll always remember. Write notes and tuck them in a scrapbook that you can look at when you feel ready.

Look for comforting things. Collect cozy objects that remind you of your loved one, like a sweatshirt, flannel shirt, or blanket. Wrap yourself up and know that every time you think about that person, they'll still be with you.

FIGHT FOR A CURE

If you lost a loved one to an illness, can you raise money to fight the disease? Take part in a charity run or walk with your family. You'll feel good knowing you're doing something to help others. And you might meet new friends—kids who know what you're going through because they have survived loss, too.

NAVIGATING THE NEWS!

The world is always changing, and news headlines can make you think it has become a really dangerous place. Why? Because news stories focus on the most dramatic events—things that don't happen very often.

Think about it: If a headline grabs your attention, you'll hit "play" on the video or share the story with a friend. That's how companies that report the news stay in business. But if those shocking stories don't happen very often, they probably *won't* happen to you. If something in the news scares you, here's how to take care of yourself.

Don't hit REPLAY

Watching scary videos over and over again can make you feel like what you're seeing happens all the time. It doesn't. Click "stop" and move on to a video that makes you smile.

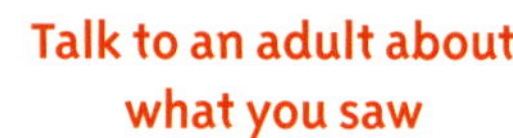

Talk to an adult about what you saw

Are you worried about violence at school? Or a natural disaster near your home? Talk to a parent, caregiver, or teacher. They'll remind you of all the people working to keep you safe at school and in your community.

Look for the heroes

Do you see people rescuing pets from floods? First responders caring for those in need? Workers clearing streets, and neighbors helping one another? Whenever bad things happen, many *good* people show up to help.

Choose your news wisely

Not every story or video you see online is true. How can you tell fact from fiction? Play detective and look for these clues:

A story to believe:

- shows you clearly who posted it—a newspaper, magazine, or news website.
- gives you quotes from real people and data from scientists or studies.
- gives you both sides of a story instead of just one point of view.

A story to shut down:

- doesn't say who wrote it or posted it. Or it sounds like the opinion of one person or group.
- might have typos or misspelled words.
- might use scary pictures or headlines in full capitals to grab your attention. If a story is trying to scare you or make you angry, it's less likely to be true.
- might be trying to sell you something or get you to sign up for something. That's an ad, not real news!

If you're not sure if a story is true, ask an adult to help you check the facts. And if you think a story might be false, *don't* share it with friends. Take charge of what you see, read, and believe—and help your friends do the same.

riding out disasters

Do you worry about having to leave your house because of a fire or a flood? Natural disasters can be so scary! You might wonder when—or if—your family will ever get back home. But there are ways to care for yourself and your family right now.

Pack a bag

- Pack the belongings that mean the most to you. Ask yourself, *Can I buy a new one if I need to?* If you can, leave it behind. Take only the treasures you know can't be replaced.
- Help younger siblings make the same choices about their special things.
- If you have a pet, help your parents pack an emergency kit for that pet:
  - ☐ A leash, collar, and carrier
  - ☐ Food, water, and medications
  - ☐ Comforting things like a bed, blanket, or toy
  - ☐ A litter box and litter for cats, or plastic bags for dog waste

Stay safe

Even after hurricanes, fires, and earthquakes pass, your neighborhood may still be dangerous. Don't wade through high waters after a flood. Don't explore buildings that have been damaged, and don't let your siblings or pets do it either. Wait until adults declare each space safe.

Be grateful for what you still have

Make a list of what and who survived the storm: your house, pets, family, friends, and neighbors. Then look around for the people who helped you get through. Make cards or say thank you to police officers, firefighters, and other responders.

Help others

- Pass out water or snacks to people who come to clean up.
- Share what you have with neighbors whose things were destroyed.
- Give your family lots of hugs. After a disaster, a little extra kindness goes a long way.
- Give your pets love and reassurance. Change is just as hard for them as it is for you. And calming a pet will keep *you* calm, too.

BIG truth

When you ride out a storm, you tap into your resilience. You're stronger now than before. You know what matters most, and you'll be better able to handle whatever comes your way.

10 ways to care for yourself RIGHT NOW

1. Step outside or sit near a window

Sunshine helps your body make chemicals that can help you feel happier and less stressed. Any natural light helps, even on a cloudy day.

2. Move your body

It'll boost your mood, too. Make up a dance, take your pet for a walk (or run), or see how many sit-ups you can do in a row.

3. Set a mini goal

Try saying a tongue twister three times without messing up, or holding a plank for a full minute. Every time you reach a goal, you prove to yourself that you *can* do hard things.

4. Compliment yourself

Name five things you like about you: Maybe you're a good listener, or you draw horses really well. Maybe you're great at telling jokes, or you're an excellent speller. No one shares all of your skills and talents. You're one of a kind!

5. "Visit" your happy place

Close your eyes and imagine yourself in a relaxing place, such as in the branches of a tree or on a blanket on the beach. Describe what you can see, hear, feel, and smell. Make the place feel real, and you'll be able to "travel" there whenever you're feeling angry, upset, or anxious.

6. Take three balloon breaths

Count to three as you slowly breathe in, feeling your stomach rise like a balloon. Hold your breath for three seconds, and then slowly blow it back out for three.

7. Do one thing that scares you just a little

Try a new food. Brave the basement with a flashlight. Invite a new friend to sleep over. Every time you face a fear (even a small one), your confidence grows.

8. Put down your phone or tablet

Then pick *up* a book, craft, or board game. Ask someone in your family to join you. Face-to-face is still the best way to connect!

9. Be kind to someone

Compliment a friend. Make a card for a teacher. Bring brownies to a neighbor. Making someone happy makes *you* feel happier, too.

10. List three people or things you're grateful for

Maybe it's a grandparent, your pet, and a rainbow you saw today. Taking time to be grateful boosts happiness—it's a fact!

BIG truth

Caring for yourself is something you'll do for a lifetime. Sometimes you'll feel happy and healthy, other times you may not. But now you know how to reach out to parents and caregivers when you need help. You have tricks you can use to get back to good—and you're smart and strong enough to use them.

Write to us:

Caring for Herself Editor
American Girl
333 Continental Blvd.
El Segundo, CA 90245

All comments and suggestions received by American Girl may be used without compensation or acknowledgment. We're sorry, but we are not able to return photos.

Here are some other American Girl books you might like:

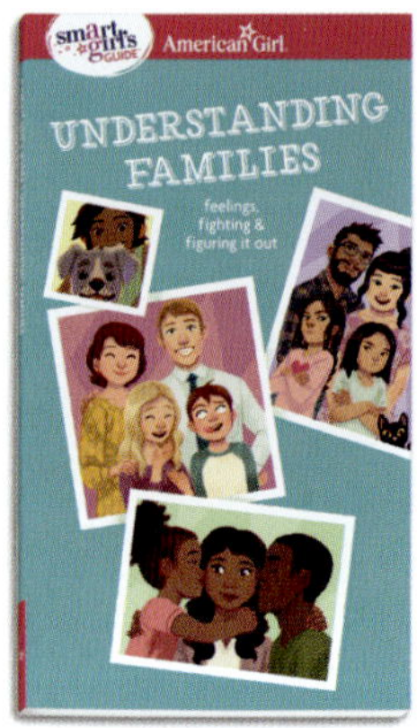

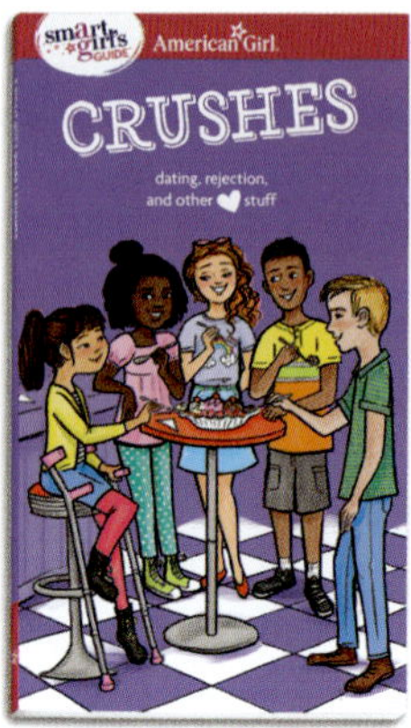

Each sold separately. Find more books online at americangirl.com.

Parents, request a FREE catalog at **americangirl.com/catalog.** Sign up at **americangirl.com/email** to receive the latest news and exclusive offers.